Brothers of Morning

for Alyssa, my daughter

Brothers of Morning

poems

Martin Steingesser

A DEERBROOK EDITION
2002

PUBLISHED BY
Deerbrook Editions
P.O.Box 542
Cumberland, Maine 04021-0542

FIRST EDITION

ISBN number: 0-9712488-0-X

Manufactured in the United States of America

Book Design by Jeffrey Haste

Brothers of Morning

Call it desire

to make a life
out of all I had,

a handful of feathers
surrounding

a body of air
I whispered into, *birrrd—*

from "The Birds That Are Not in Our Hands,"—L.R. Berger

CONTENTS

Another Country

Attempting Flight

Red Dust

Brothers of Morning

Another Country

... the way it is in love, every poem
life in another country

A Bell

            calls the heart to be still, a friend
told me. I hear how
                it speaks of a center. I listen, thinking
everything is held in each soft toll, so
like breath, opening through the moment
                        .   already gone.

There is an owl, the bird book tells,
                     the boreal, that's
a soundless bell of feathers all but some weeks
a year, when he tolls, calling a mate. Imagine

dark pines, spruces, yes, the owl moon now
full, dropping blue and white feathers
over the snow, the heart hungry, itself
a fist-sized bell of feathers.
                  Do I lose myself

in words? And it so happens, I am called
to stillness. Can I grow
               boreal wings?—fly to you
through the black branches.

Night Letters

January 9, Saturday

I crossed Eagle Lake on skis this afternoon.
It was snowing, the Sun far ahead
                      a smudge of persimmon.

January 10, Sunday

I want to put out the light.
If you were here, I would light a candle
and look long on your face in the dark
after you closed your eyes.
I hear ice growing thick
out there on Eagle Lake.
Tonight, the bones of eagles are cracking in the lake.
I look for you, perhaps the way Eskimo watch for the Sun.
Somewhere out there you are waking, east of the light.
How beautiful, to think of you
while I am deep in this sleepless night
like all the caught, fast things in the lake.
In the morning, sunlight glances the snow
that already has lifted your eyes.
How beautiful to have you rising
among the apricot fires in the east.
I'm tired. If you were here,
I would kiss your eyelids, then fall asleep.

January 11, Monday

Everything seems impossible again
after two days walking on water.
No matter yesterday even toes
were signaling burning, bright messages.

All day it is four o'clock, the hour the Sun
does this blue trick:
                    mountains, sky, lakes, snowfields deepen,
until finally the windows are black.

Everything has become impossible.
I try to look out the window
                    and see only my reflection.
I turn for help and remember
one night you woke from a dream, sat up and said: "Begin."

January 13, Wednesday

How can I go on talking like this,
                    as if you were here?
I wake at three o'clock and, simply,
                    you aren't.
There's none of your hair for my hand to stroke
                    or fingers to tug.
You are not saying softly, "Let me sleep."
My lamp is lit,
            out in the dark it is 27 below,
and there are reflections of me
                    in five windows.
I would open them all
if these whispers here would fly
                    and touch your ear.

January 22, Friday

How you hover about the fringes of lamplight.
I put you by, reading Basho,

following far as temple pines below Matsuyama.
Still, you flutter there
                              beyond the light,
doing a fine job keeping me off Basho's Back Roads—
yourself out of reach.

January 24, Sunday

Among the pines outside my window, the dark
is so impenetrable, so final,
yet all night you are there
in the sound of melting snow.
Morning,
                    and snow is falling
like a white fawn
                              stepping into the quiet.

January 29, Friday

Twilight
                    again, everything
becoming obscure
                              except trees closeby
black
          against the snowlight.
I know I need to go out,
let the lake wind wash face and hands.
And will I find you there, in the dark cave
where lake and sky dissolve?
And, yes, maybe I'll howl,
or stand absolutely still, listening
to the colors change, listening.

February 16, Tuesday

The sky returns
before dawn, blue
moving to light, a fan

opening.
                    Trees
slowly step into color—green,
a promise kept. How

can I tell you? Something

full happens.
Day
draws its long walk

out of shadow, reaching

forward, wings
coming down, great swallowing strokes.
Legs trailing now

touch once, leaving

a ripple, only
this circle
growing, as if light

were something flying

every day.

This Longing

      . . . awoke to rain
around 2:30 this morning
thinking of you, because I'd said
only a few days before, this

is what I wanted, to lie with you in the dark
listening how rain sounds
in the tree beside my window,
on the sill, against the glass, damp

cool air on my face. I am loving
fresh smells, light flashes in the
black window, love how you are here
when you're not, knowing we will

lie close, nothing between us; and maybe
it will be still, as now, the longing
that carries us
into each other's arms

asleep, neither speaking
least it all too soon turn to morning, which
it does. Rain softens, low thunder, a car
sloshes past.

Awake at 5:04, which is

also the house number where I was born and grew up. I don't know
what that means, except I am starting again this morning from bed
and the dark. I return to what you said. I can't help myself, you rub me
the right way, like music sticks, how crickets sing, like katydids, the green
True Katydid on the postage stamp that brought your last letter. Colors
fall in step for you, like the fabric you stitched
to carry the yellow birch flute I play. "This is from Africa," you said,
pointing at a zagzig, black and gold pattern. "This from Bali, the ochre
and burnt orange silk from India." Batik fish swim by without clothes,
and the Moon crawls sideways to the Sun. Everything's changed. Are grouse
underwater this autumn? You can't hear their mating song, you tell me,
but feel it through your breastbone, the same place you've gone and moved in
on me, which is where I hear yours. Everything's changed. I'm picking katydids
and swallowtails out of my mailbox. It's a new picture, another country.
You tell of a fox playing with a puppy, rolling a ball—Was it the Sun,
the Moon between them? "Look, how wonderful," you said, "where domestic
and wild meet."
                    "Isn't that love?" I couldn't help saying.
"Yes," you said, sitting up, bare shoulders against window light, paling
stars and those first, dull *thud thuds* of the hunters around us.

Fall Back

The clock at last got into the wind,
The world at last got out of itself.

. . . .

At last we can make sense, you and I.
　　　　　　　　—*Laura Riding*

　　　　　　　　up too early. Again
the middle of the night, morning, whichever
so I'm back to this conversation, how love
arrives, appears found—
seed we husk, plant and
replant in each other, in ourselves
not unlike poems.
　　　　　　　　Lips
tongues, planting in the dark
breath of skin, the black fur
parting, come cries
of being whole
of being separate
of being one
of being one in all the feeling—this
talk of sex, how I feel in you
was missing.

　　　　　　　　This morning, to tell the truth
what I want
is to go back to sleep
only it's too late, the extra hour
setting back the clock
someone last night promised won't help
the bedroom window
already filling in morning light, and I'm up
in praise of sex, love in our bodies
like you said thunder

and lightning in your heart and sometimes nothing
seeming to matter as much as skin on skin
intelligence of touch, no sweetness
without stain, and I think how you told me
fucking wasn't in your computer dictionary, only
cuckooing, bucking, sucking . . . and remember
the church's word immaculate, without spots
and love the way kids know
not to stay out of the mud
yes, the wind has got in the clock
sun in all my rooms! I'll never get back to sleep last night
so now say back to you
what you said laughing out loud
about the dictionary   and fucking—

                                        I cuckoo to you.

For the Moment

We couldn't stay, any more
Than the light. . .
—*Joe Bolton*

A loud boat horn

somewhere, despite how clear it is; crows;
an airplane engine; the digestive groan
and clank of a garbage truck, my Chinese palm
afire in sun greens and yellows. Be still,

I tell myself. Sunlight
                         fills my living space. Light
splinters, swimming in among rib bones. The sun
pulls south, the room suddenly cool, like shade
and air beside a waterfall. And here

                              is my love,
covers rumpled where already she's risen, now
standing in her doorway, trying on this morning's
soft, early yellows . . .
                         Wind, just enough to lift

her good colors, and there is a shower of light,
like a sudden yellow rain I once watched
along a shoreline of aspen, lake and sky, the leaves
and reflections falling

The Voice I Want

"Goodnight," I said, looking through my window, past Orion,
the Seven Sisters, through the studio
to your bed, windows of dark trees and stars all around.
How can I live in one place?
I want to be with you and not with you.
How is it talking to you when not here
I hear the voice I want?

                         Fish rise in me, mouths angling upward
to light . . .
            Another woman lives in my house.

Yet I am here, first snow flurries
salting the wings of surprised pigeons, thinking of you,
a commotion of silk as you work, searching colors
and patterns of yearning in your studio.
                     And this is my work, too.

Reluctantly, I admit some deep-felt ache, sometimes
joy, is shared only in the heart's faith.
Why is this often so difficult? Yet
moments we've had, riding
leaf-blown hills, tight curves on the motorcycle—
or nothing under us, riding nothing
but our bodies' breathless rushes.
I love you in my arms.
The woman in me is jealous. How
                 do I live with you both?
There is no bottom to this. At the same time, I am among the silt
and currents of all my losses. Swim with me.
Run with me. (If I mix metaphors,
then I mix them.) What is it wanting to love
like this?—running through wet grasses, no clothes on.

After You Left

How do I orient
                    among our star crowd—your asteroids,
my satellites, the planets? . . .

I am not going to cry over this.

                              Pisces—oh,
my Sun sign! I have been in this space enough to notice
no one is swimming with me
down here, no matter how many whichways at once. I love
my Pisces nature but not always the heart crush
I do in these blue, slow waters.

                         But no, I won't cry
if you bail out of this ocean I want so bodily to swim with you.

          I didn't know you were drowning
when I went out and bought the bigger futon
and set of black, full-size sheets, the form-fitting lower with
black on black wavy lines, for us to have more room to swim
together, apart, however the waters pull, everywhichway we wanted.

No, I am not going to cry over this. I'm going to crop my hair,
I am going to go upside down on my hands again.

The night you left, I woke after a short sleep, and at first could feel only
how sore I was from two days hammering work. I got up—
oh, aching, and before I could revise, rewrite
whatever is happening between us, how light
I grew. Maybe another gift of this affair finally will be
a bigger bed—the better to rest? better to dream? the better
to rise into a bigger life? I love my new bed.

No, I'm not going to wring hands
over this. I am going to stand on them till I get it right and kneel
only before music makers. And the music. Circles I enter
will be for the *jôgo*, the game—to dance, sometimes meet.

All this to tell you,
despite the joy I bring, I'm from the other side of your life, the side
you've been keeping out, in the dark, yes, the owl
flying at your window, beating wings against the panes.

"Again?

again   again   you'll see
it's easy   begin again   long ago"
—*Grace Paley*

What voice is lifting and bending long grasses, burnt
gold and green in the sunlight? All my life I have searched,
yearning for these fields, rustlings of light and umber.

∞

It surprises me sometimes
                    finding her gone.

∞

                              I hold most dear
her dance, imagining gestures, each one a moment, a song
from below the breastbone, the way flight
                              begins in the heart.

∞

If it isn't love brushing the blue, smooth fur of the lake
with the back of a hand, what then?

∞

                         This morning, rain.
A damp wind through the window, upstairs someone steps
across the floor.
             Love, we have put fresh paint on all the walls,
the floorboards shine.

Acquainted with Night

"O star . . .
Some mystery becomes the proud.
But to be wholly taciturn
In your reserve is not allowed."
—*Robert Frost*

I wake in the cold-gripped, early dark and shut off the radio—that moment
Silent Night on the breath of muted horns and a choir. Now only night,
    patches of snow

bright under streetlamps. At my bay window, I could be standing watch,
    plotting this city's course.
Someone is crossing the park, walking so purposefully. Maybe it's the hour, or
    the cold, or both.

There are headlights and sounds of tires and wind going past. I think north,
    then east along the
interstate, over the Kennebec, following the new bridge's long arc. Not far, out
    toward the coast,

a woman I once loved wakes, comes downstairs and stands, looking from her
    door
into this morning's constellations. I know how she likes the unyielding,
    sleepless stars,

keeps a telescope there. The better to listen, she smiles. One time we caught
    the Leonides, those
shooting lights. I think of Frost, quarreling with their distances. "Always, we
    are somewhere

for many things," that lover told me—"only we narrow the field,
        grasping just one
or a few." And I am wanting to drive past acceleration highways,the
        heart-shrinking distances

and my restless body, to how we are held, not unlike these revolving, old
        families of stars.

Attempting Flight

... the great dark birds of history screamed and plunged
into our personal weather.
—*Adrienne Rich*

... to anyone listening in the dark ... Let me hear you
by any means: by horn. by fever, by night, even by some poem

attempting flight home.
—*Joy Harjo*

Woman Behind the Wheel in Sunlight

January 1987

I don't know where I was, didn't understand the driver
who honked, holding one thumb up as he passed
going the other way. I had hiked miles through what
the earthquake left over a decade before, sun and dust
of Managua in my mouth. I was seeing for myself, out shopping
for signs of the victorious revolution—smiles full of teeth,
the revolutionary murals: Liberty topless, coming over
the barricades, rifle in hand, the people's colors
lifted in the other, leading a charge against whirlybirds
and rockets . . . Here were vacant lots—what it means to kick
against a central bank—abandoned Chevys
and Fords, some with no doors, the rooftops rusted out.
In one, a woman sat behind the wheel, her breasts
beautiful and young in sunlight. More, all 16 or 17, lounged
without clothes about the cars. A man stood among them
smoking, following me.

                              I don't know who they were.
The woman behind the wheel looked like one of Gauguin's
umber nudes. It was hot, miles from anywhere.
Lie down in the back seat, her smile kept saying. Suddenly

Nicaragua, all our dismal interventions—how
we back the wrong side for bananas, again democracy for the
dictators—
                 suddenly the isms, the money
politics bare-assed in sunlight, down to dusky
skin, rust, broken glass.
                     Me, dust settled my mouth, want
and guilt arguing in my stomach. I wished

I'd had more Spanish, hadn't felt
such a gringo. What if I entered
their naked lives, had touched—been touched
by one of them some way I wasn't taught to rejoice in.

This is a Safe House

for Anna Calero de Lopez
Nicaragua Libre 1987

she wants you to know,
               even back when the Guardia
shot people on the streets,
bloodying all Masaya, the streets
held in the red eye
               of the sniper's scope.
Step through her door
and let hands open,
               the body breathe,
let the heart's muscle
               unknot.

She wants you to know, at Anna's
you eat the cool, green light of the cucumber,
then lie down, drawing around you
violet shadows
               the color of dark beets;
you curl into sleep, filling space like air,
moving without weight,
               gathering losses,
old wounds huffing through blood
like blind, tunneling animals.

In the morning, you blink
at how sunlight
               surrounds each leaf,
at the way voices travel like light:—
               and Anna,
herself a new morning
               in clean cottons,

handmaid of the earth's cup,
                                   this river
of black beans, fried banana, coffee. . .
this Anna laughs,
                         showing one gold tooth.

No Ducks

February 1987

"Perhaps literature may help to preserve
the true name of each thing."

—*Eduardo Galeano*

"Ducks!" our President said, speaking out about revolutionaries in Nicaragua.
　　"They walk like them, talk like them, they're ducks!"—meaning,
　　I suppose, something like red is red is red.
Now, I went to Nicaragua and did not see one duck, sitting or otherwise.
I did see Southern constellations, leaning a bit to the left.
I did see passion-red tropical flowers and a billboard saying, NICARAGUA IS
　　ALL HEART. (*Corazon*, written in red.)
There were newsboys without shoes hawking at traffic lights in Managua.
I watched women on street corners selling papaya, watermelon, golden slices
　　of mango; saw their sure, swift hands, their tired eyes.
I saw the clean, bare streets and faded pink walls in Granada; sat on a park
　　bench among palm rustlings in the early
　　morning, watching people walk to work; saw their freshly laundered
　　colors and well-combed, often wet hair so black in the sun.
Saw the volcano giants Motombo and Momotombito framed by low terra cotta
　　rooftops.
I saw an old man drive by in a horse-drawn cart with wooden wheels, then a
　　small pickup truck carrying two horses.
In Masaya, Anna Calero served the same *platano* and *chillote* she'd fed
　　freedom fighters hiding from the dictator, Somoza.
I heard her say, "Here no one surrenders. We keep clear the vision of the
　　Revolution."
I saw a statue of one of their martyrs, Andreas Castro, facing north, a stone in
　　hand like one he threw at American
buccaneer William Walker more than a century before, ready to throw again.
Everywhere on walls, I saw how people speak to martyrs of the revolution:
　　CARLOS,WE'RE GETTING THERE: JULIO
　　WE HAVE NOT FORGOTTEN.
I met, without appointment, the Minister of Culture, poet Ernesto Cardenal,

who bestowed on me like a benediction his smile.
Watched the general of the army pass closer than our own Secretary of
     Defense dares walk among strangers without protection of guards.
I heard a commander address a group of coffee workers, telling them the
     people of our states are good.
Saw soldiers standing guard, walking about. "*Mi amigo*," one facing me said,
     eyes narrowing,
Not once did I hear, "*Yanqui!* go home."
                                        Nowhere were there any ducks.
Only occasionally I was told, "You are not American."
"North American," I was reminded. "You are North American."

The Disappeared

I heard about a woman of El Salvador
whose tongue was cut out
                        for asking after her daughter,
one of the disappeared in her village.
She asks us, "Where in the dust
have they flung my daughter
                        or my tongue?"
I am mindful how
                my thoughts about her circle.
The summer night is loud with stars, and there is music
and clapping just down the road. Somewhere
the other side of night, my own daughter
is waking. I don't know on what her eyes light
when they open, only that the birds
                                surely sing in them.
Standing now under the astonishing stars, I think—
In what tongue does one summon daughters?
Sure as words spin out,
the birds this morning fly in my daughter's eyes.

Brother

"Think of it: the worlds in this world."

—*Laure-Anne Bosselaar*

"The past is never dead. It isn't even past."

—*William Faulkner*

Always, I was looking from six years back, wishing
Lewis would reach an arm around my shoulder, teach me how he charmed
the ball. I watch him now, bald, overweight, swiftness gone to light
and love in the fingers, crowning my tooth, nothing said—

Needles and sharp metal sparkle.
                              Some other time, I can't help thinking,
in another country he'd be someone hurting me. Mouth open, I follow the
          easy way
he handles instruments, moving among jars, solvents, a trumpet solo
tooling on the radio. Charlie Bird, he played horn, and angels
hushed. We don't speak. Dipping into something red, Lewis brushes a tooth,

and I am thinking of this army private, toothless grin in his black face
years after the massacre at My Lai, a newsman asking why
he didn't shoot like the others.
                              "My mama taught me," he said,
"things you don't do."

          "Relax the cheek," my brother says, the gold coming up
brighter than anything, and at once remember wrestling, Lewis without warning
punching me hard in the mouth.

   Mothers wring their hands, wailing
beside small coffins in Nicaragua. Late 80's, our president telling us they're
savages, said they had no feelings. Years before, the dictator we banked there
comes back to the dinner table, blood on his white shirt.
                              Inside this poem

I can't pull the bad tooth—or better, carve new ones. That fist
surprised the hell out of me, and how my lip didn't hurt, and someplace else
I couldn't locate did—

        how we turn, walk away, saying nothing.

Shofar

On the night of November 25, 1987, a Palestinian boy, armed with a few
grenades, light machinegun and pistol, flew a small, kite-like aircraft through
a security zone into an Israeli military compound. He attacked the barracks
and was killed in a firefight with the soldiers. Within days, an uprising against
Israel's 21 years of enforced occupation erupted among the refugee camps
in Gaza and the West Bank.

for Kamal Boullata

I can't believe how far it has gotten from where we met, restless now
     in the blood light of autumn, listening to traffic beyond the window,
     watching the cats preen.
I think of you Kamal, refugee in our land of refugees that no longer wants
     refugees.
Palestinians were forbidden even to paint a homeland: "All the artists went
to jail," you said, and in Jerusalem told the Israelis—"Fascism!"

This is the season we met, in the Adirondacks, green going yellow and red,
     what is changing constant.
"When you look at one thing, say this leaf," you said, "and suddenly know
     its secret and understand everything—when something you know is
     beautiful, like that leaf, which suddenly is even more beautiful, that is
     Allah akbar!—more wonderful than god."

Yes, I think of you, and think I know, how we are joined underneath, not
     unlike the trees, yet still am confounded by the country between us.
For how many native peoples: Arawak, Lakono, Mayan, Nootka, Innuit,
     Aleut, Zuni—for how many who step to a smaller drum, or who won't
     march, has it been too late?
Now the harvests of profit fill our plate. Now uranium tailings ride the Plains'
     winds. Now the dark bud of melanoma blooms on the hand, or cheek.

Let's go to the movies, go to bed, go to work, go to lunch. Leave the road kills
     where they lie, this is America, land of plenty, home of the free.

Sometimes I do imagine a line joining everything, imagine pulling on it and
      watchingevery dark face rise and turn to the light, the way a whole
      field of giant sunflowers I saw once in a setting sun blare out like the
      Leonora Overture.

Do I dress misfortune—another's—in the good clothing of words?

How do I apologize for what betrays me?

Think of the boy who inflamed the *intifada*, the Palestinian shout for freedom,
      flying a homemade glider through air defenses of the Israeli army to
      set foot finally for the first time in his ancestral land,
      and how not think—*David*!

I Keep Thinking of You, Victor Jara

September 11, 1973

It's as if really I were there,
hearing the vowels of his red notes lift in the air
as big as blood oranges.
We are all still there, we are all arrested
in that night, filling the grandstands of Estadio Chile in Santiago
while the commandante mimics him, making motions as if strumming a guitar.
The soldiers want to put an end to such playing
and before us hold out his arms
and in two blows with an ax chop off the fingers of both hands.
Yet he stands up, and he sings—
                        we singing with him
until the stadium thickens with song like the voice of an army.
What could they do? What can soldiers do
after beating with rifle butts,
                  after cutting off fingers?
What could they do when singing, his singing went on
like fingers that go on playing without a hand,
like a heart that goes on beating without a body?
What could they do to silence him but shoot?

Victor, before you I swear
                  never to shut up.
I add this song to yours,
                  and curse you colonels of Chile, curse you
senators and presidents of death
                  with the fingers of Victor Jara.

Those Pelicans

to Pablo Neruda
Santiago, Chile
23 September 1973

Soldiers pacing the corridor
outside your hospital room:
a band of boots
                    to ring you out.
And you,
        lying there
drinking glucose in your veins,
plotting poems.
                    They know,
they know, those generals
itching to get you.
And you know what they won't forgive?
Joy! just as you said, on your words joy
came over to our side.

They say you wrote with a white mountain,
and while you sang a white star
circled above your hand
like a pelican bringing in the mail.
No one can stop them, Pablo—
                        those pelicans
coming back and forth.

The Three

for Miroslav Kosek, 12, Hanus Löwy, 13, and Bachner,
three children who died in German concentration camps

Koleba, you signed your dreams,
raids over the wall
           for green meadow smell
and the warm hum of bees.
You craved these, not like sweets
                        but the way fawns forage snow for shoots,
and so under one name
              wrote other lives, brilliant as air
burning like a star
          over Terezín, over Prague.

And your voices—such thin arms!
                 straws across the holocaust,
reeds weaving into light
            under this sign, your star
       pulses
            Ko-le-ba
                   pulses
bright yellow, a burr
        —your star in the throat of death.

Love Canal

It's the channel babies swim
into the world.
Black, Red, Yellow, White—
we all swim it.
And Lord! when we surface this side
and gulp our first crazy mouthful—*Air!*
it's there,
we've come up clean.

And you know what hooker is.
That's a word for who sells
love canal.
And what happens?
Well, business.
There's a time you're young.
You're lucky, things go your way.
You look good.
The Johns (a name for the man
who trades in what's free)
love you.

No one sees.
Sometimes it won't show up for weeks,
sometimes not for 10 years, or more.
Sometimes it won't show up at all,
till some kid swimming the canal
doesn't come up clean.

Money Medicine Poem

$11.3 million, what does James Mellor of General Dynamics do with it?
In how many beds does he sleep?
I want to know, how many breakfasts does he eat?
$11.3 million—that is every year, year after year.
What does he do with it?
James, how many copy machines do you have?
How many shredders?
Do you keep one in the bathroom?
How many suits do you own?
How many closets for the secrets money keeps?
Secrets? Does money keep secrets?
Year after year, 11.3 million.
Why so much in corporate pockets?
I need a chant to bring dollars back in my life.

Om Bram Brie Hasti Paté Yea Na Ma Om

I need a moon to draw the oceans of money back.
What does AT&T executive Bob Allen do with $9 million in stock options?
It's a great system we have.
Secrets? What secrets?
AT&T lays off 40,000 workers.
Robert Allen, you must feel like a god.
Robert Allen gets $9 million.
What are you building out of our conversations?
What is your phone number, anyway?
Will you answer a call?

Om Bram Brie Hasti Paté Yea Na Ma Om

How do we reach corporate dynamos to buy girl scout cookies?
How do we call when we want to rent a bus for the school picnic?
How do we call when the soup kitchen's out of soup?
How come big bucks stuff so few pockets?

It's a wonderful system we've got, all our money on the top floor,
corporate executives calling the truths we live.
Families of gods, like up on Mount Olympus, great scraperskies of CEOs.
One of them markets 100% water for juice;
another mainlines cigarettes;
another the medicines for smokers;
another pumps cancer into rivers and lakes, into oceans of air;
another lobbies for tax breaks to clean up the mess.
Great system we've got, billions stuffed in so few pockets.
I want a chant to bring the dollars back.

Om Bram Brie Hasti Paté Yea Na Ma Om

Give me those pants with money pockets,
closetsful of pants, big bucks in the pockets.
Lean back, feet up, have a million dollar stogie,
blow giant smoke rings over Broadway.
I want a chant, put the moon back in my pocket.

Stilt Dancing the Penacook Valley Parade
in What Must Be Heaven

for Wesley McNair

How to tell what happened that summer morning, marching Main Street
Rumford, everywhere smelling like rotten eggs? ("Hydrogen sulfide,"
I overheard this bystander say.) How to explain the sinking
feeling, eyeing the one float from WE CARE DAY CARE with a dozen kids
in bikinis, pink umbrella and handfuls of sand, as I sat on the car roof tying
on stilts? Or else define the tagrag Paresseux Marching Band of snare drums,
tom tom and one bass; color guard of American, Canadian and Maine
flags, then Jon Richard and his daughter on the purple Harley, followed
by a player-piano-sounding calliope, pealing out Semper Fidelis. "Parades
are up there with apple pie," Dorie, the 20-something organizer, said.
"I have this simple philosophy," she said, "all this negative shit has to go."
I'm not sure what she was referring to, the poor turn out or thick, clean-looking
white billowing out of Boise Cascade, twin red-trimmed stacks
poking right up into what had to be summer's best
china blue. All this beside the rolling Androscoggin, and Denise and Sandee
Welch, Steve Gallant, Davie Frost, Debi and David Briggs beat the drums, for the
Penacook Valley Festival Parade has begun, and suddenly
I want to cheer, because something about Keith Sinclair—the way he steps
out in the color guard makes me think he would shine if the rifle
he shoulders were a broom, and what could I do but take off, whirling and
kicking for the sky, everybody marching solemn-faced together, this surprise
fanfare of the heart, the flags an Androscoggin of red, blue, green, yellow
through back streets and main; and we marched for two kids on
the hood of a car, for elders in robes waving behind screen doors, past the blue
fire hydrant, and I danced for one girl with her puppy, for a man
across a vacant lot, a blue dress blowing on a clothesline. It doesn't matter
streets were empty, they came to windows, left TVs flickering in empty rooms,
came out of the hardware store and Kohler's Plumbing, groups on corners
clapping, eyeglasses filling with light. It doesn't matter in a smaller moment
I didn't want to be part of their parade. Judy Willett hit the cymbals, eyes smiled
up at me, we met somewhere we knew each other before we knew,

        roadside weeds
broke out in fragrance, something threading the streets threading us, morning's
first swagger of heat staggering back. Drums beat, *Smash the TV!* Drums beat,
Take back the river! the air—
                        Come out! Come out! the drums beat.

Red Dust

. . . but who is it now in my ear who hears with my voice?
Who says words with my mouth?
—Rumi

China, Maine

Suddenly the rain stops.
All around the lake
trees and mountains quietly double.
Mottled trout swim among the slender aspen
and birch.
A cricket chirps like six,
the brook rushes louder.
Yet only the highest branches
in the tallest maple stir.
A leaf falls,
                        another,
        then many—
one never knows.
Some breeze enters
the heart's ear,
ruffling its red fur.
In the grass
among red and yellow leaves
the old life sings.

Fishing

"Sometimes words come hard—they resist me
till I pluck them from deep water like hooked fish. . ."
—Lu Ji (261-303)

You have to be willing
to wait days and days with nothing
biting.
            Wait

while the far leaves, the sky change
blues and greens, and birdcalls,
wind, river become the sound of thinking.
This line you cast
                reaches into different music.

A murmur flutters over the water—
                be more still . . .

Sometimes a moment happens
                when what moves
doesn't, when the trees and grasses
along the riverbank seem to hold their breath,
and it is the stones that breathe . . .

                The fish you want
is rising in another world.

'El Condor Pasa'

Wind of light out of the south, the high, sunswept
Andes—and in all the rooms of my loneliness I am thinking—
How to speak?
I don't know how to begin, and I know
I cannot tell you
feelings moving through me
like herds of deer through wild grasses.
Lift!
just lift, this wind says, as if
that's all there is to it,
as if I could grow wings
thinking about it. Where
is the language of feathers? —words to distance walls
and soar? speech
like the flight of the condor?
Once I heard—Listen, I swear
all the vast Andes breathe in a song.
O desolation, high
plains of wind, thin, transparent waters of spirit, years of snow and light,
open green wings, lift
on the flute's breath.

Anonymous

I know a poem of six lines that no one knows
who wrote, except
                that the poet was Chinese and lived
centuries before the birth of
Christ. I said it aloud
                once to some children, and when I reached
the last line suddenly they
understood and together all went—*"Ooo!"*

Imagine that poem, written
                by a poet truly
who is Anonymous, since
                in the strict corporeal sense
he hasn't existed for thousands of years—imagine! his small poem
                                traveling
without gas or even a single grease job
across centuries of space and a million
miles of time
                to me, who spoke it
softly aloud to a group of children who heard
and suddenly all together
                cried *"Ooo!"*

In Response

". . . science fiction or horror, not poetry, which has limited appeal."

—*a science fiction writer*

There is talk going around I am esoterik, or maybe some
doily thing for the fat arms of couches—self-indulgent, prim,
correct—in other words, dead. Maybe. All this talk, this
funeral of gossip, when always I am so close, near
as a heartbeat, keeping time in the pockets of commuters, winking
by in broadcasts of fast pitches. No use, no use, here I am,
like memory, plumb in the uprights, dependable as pain, smiling
like keys under your belt. You might as well try to do away
with grit, or the milky rivers of stars. And it's no use
calling names like rondeau, sonnet, sestina. I am red ochre
in the thighbone of a Bantu and rust burning in your new Ford.
Forget me, and you have found me, the first green threading
January snow. *Snow?* Yeah! let's knock off a few hats. Maybe
you hardly know what I mean. Good health to you, anyway.

Shoplifting Poetry

We're in the bookstore stealing poems,
lifting the best lines.
You cop one from Williams,
I stick my hand into Pound.
No one's looking—
I throw you a line from *The Cantos*.
It disappears in your ear like spaghetti.
We stuff ourselves with Crane,
cummings, Lowell, Voznesensky—
Neruda, Rilke, Yeats!
The goods dissolve in our brain.
Now we move from the shelves with caution.
The cashier's watching. Can she tell?
Fat! We've overeaten.
You giggle. End-rhymes leak at your lips like bubbles.
I clap a hand on your mouth.
You are holding my ears
as we fall out the door.

Painting 101

for Abby Shahn

"Fuck the painting," she said, her brush working.
                                        Me, I wanted to keep
what we had. Anyway,
                    I was out of fresh moves. Too much
was happening—black crosses flying over, small fires breaking out,
crop circles turning up, sudden riffs of stones
smoother than jazz.
                    Abby kept painting, moving green
across borders, quick strokes parting worlds, marrying energies—
I couldn't take it, this white wheel at the center picking up speed, everything
feeling like Franz Marc's red horses about to escape the barn, and yes
I wanted to slam shut the gate before they left the page.
"Maybe we ought to stop," I said.
                                "Fuck the painting,
it's wreck and rescue!" she said, riding past bareback
on a red Clydesdale. I grabbed her shirttails, and we leaped
the fences together, big country under our brushes.

"Whatever You Want,"

                I tell this fourth grader, who wants to know what to do.
"In my poem," I say, "gorilla is spelled r-o-s-e."
                        He is bewildered. Everyone
has started writing, even the friends he was fooling with.
Now he is out there with no support, unsure
                        which way to go.
"A rose is not a gorilla," he says.
                "I spell it how I want," I tell him.
"This is startin' to sound
              like one of those stories," he says.
"Just wait—" I write on the page between us,
"I spell Brandon, S-u-p-e-r-h-e-r-o."
"I'm a Superhero," he laughs, and adds, "I spell fox, Y-M-V-L-E!"
"What's that?" I ask.
           "I don't know," he says, pleased with himself.
"Hummingbird Junction," I throw back.
              "Dirty recess," he says, heating up,
beginning to sound like one of those beat poets.
I pitch again—"Cross-eyed sharpshooters."
"Sumo wrestlers," he says, eyes narrowing.
"Okay, bail out," I say, folding our paper into an airplane
and sticking it in the backpack on his desk. He looks at me.
                   "Ha!" I say,
"I just stuffed your pack with a gorilla, a rose, Superhero, sharpshooters,
sumo wrestlers, your fox and one Y-M-V-L-E."
                  The other kids,
also finished, start queuing up for lunch. Brandon is digging
in his pack, after the poem, which—who knows—just might fly.

Red Dust

"The shape nearest shapelessness
awes us most, suggesting the goddess."

Always, she carved the red stone.
This is one thing made me notice.
First, it was a red fish;
then a red bird, a red heron
stalking in red eel grass;
even a red madawaska;
and faces of people she knew,
including her own face red.
I came to know her this way,
as if born of red stone.
Soon, though, she began carving strange things:
red clouds rolling like symphonies
and wind sleeping in red sneakers.
One day the sky went utterly clear,
blue-clear as a door with no door.
She put down her hammer.
You could hear her eyes listening.
That's when she carved the strangest yet—
things with no names!
She's covered in the dust of them.

Brothers of Morning

A poem should always have birds in it.
Kingfishers, say, with their bold eyes and gaudy wings.
Rivers are pleasant, and of course trees.
A waterfall, or if that's not possible, a fountain rising and falling.
—*Mary Oliver*

I'm like a bird from another continent, sitting in this aviary.
The day is coming when I fly off . . .
—*Rumi*

Awake

"It's true, someone hidden controls the world;
with that being you sink or float."
—*Sikong Tu (837-908)*

The full moon is out, insistent
like that truck grinding on the hill.
Distant pines dark against the sky
are the manes of black horses.
My thoughts, like the owl in the air—

The black horses stand and listen.

The moon comes right down, breathing
cold light on my hands.

We are here
              like the moon,
like the dark pines,
                      like the owl.
We watch the black horses;
a breeze, and their ears cock—

Brothers of Morning Brush My Eyes

Sun coming up full in the rearview mirror, traveling through Hope,
    Liberty, Palermo, South China, West Paris, kids along the road,
    standing around, kicking stones, sunrise on their faces,

Myself crisscrossing the state, heading for classrooms of these same young
    lights of Portland, Presque Isle, Jackman, Monhegan, Lubec.

Lucky man, I tell myself, no joining the dots, no filling spaces on
    other people's clocks.
I'm a lucky man, afoot with a vision, tooling along, stereo tuned and
    balanced, the spring highway turning to black gold.

Now a red-tailed hawk, another—three! arpeggios of lift, brothers
    of morning, I salute you, this green moment and surrounding
    mountains our only nest.

Three hundred horses, Percherons of pistons and fire running at
    breakneck, and I have them by the wheel,

Saddlebags stuffed with poems, Walt Whitman beside me on the front
    seat, windows wide open, sunup and stars blowing out of his
    beard, and Yes!

Morning laughs for us, the open road spinning our wheels, we're
    riding the big Earth and together lean on the horn, sounding
    our barbaric honk and yahonk!

Today, the Traffic Signals
All Changed for Me

"... all beautiful golden sunflowers
...under the shadow
of the mad locomotive riverbank sunset Frisco hilly tincan
evening sitdown vision."

from "Sunflower Sutra," Allen Ginsberg

It's all language, I am thinking
on my way over the drawbridge to South Portland,
driving into a wishbone blue, autumn sky, maple
red, aspen yellow—oaks, evergreens
stretching out in sunlight. Isn't this all
message and sign, singing to us?
When I open ears, listen with eyes
wide open, the world tumbles in, suddenly
a rush through my body, how tires zummmmm
across bridge grating, sending vibratos
along limbs, out fingers
and toes. Even these dead things
we make: cement walkways,
macadam streets, all our brick and steel
and rubber, even these are alive. Sometimes
I feel so empty. Today, I am filling up, the way
this Indian Summer morning keeps fattening
on sunlight, feelings, words frothing
like yeast. Blue sky rises in my blood, geese
and monarchs migrating through; my love's an open field,
meadows of goldfinch, Anne's lace, new moon
and crow laughing . . . Tornadoes
collapse in a breath, oceans curl at my toes, galaxies
exploding in my heart. Am I going loco? I pull over
onto the roadside, cars and trucks whizzing by.
I can't get places I thought I was going. I think of old Walt,
quadrupeds and birds stucco'd all over. Why not?
And you, too, Allen, gay, locomotive sunflower laureate,

both of you, among the leaves, in all your all-star
colors, hitting all the curves, belting poems
out of the century. O look!—this is what's happening.

Skydreaming a Sunny Afternoon in Portland, a Small City

A silver needle
        angling down—
here come the wheels,
the wings dip
        ev-er so slightly, the pilot
trying to get a feel of them,
                a little like treading water.
A pilot, flying that plane I could pluck from the sky
and thread with a blue thread.
People in it, too,
           in rows of two like eggs in a crate,
and the plane going—
           flying! hundreds of miles an hour,
and looking to me like slow motion,
               floating home to Portland Airport.
And the passengers sitting,
           hands folded in laps over safety belts,
looking out through windows so small
               I can't see them,
and each one a whole traffic jam of shoes, work, breakfasts,
of paychecks, luggage, dancing, keys, laundry,
so that how they sit inside a silver needle
I could sew the button on my pants with—

Now I've lost it,
dropped somewhere down there in Portland.

Out of the Blue

On August 7, 1974, Philippe Petit performed on a cable
rigged between the towers of New York's World Trade Center.

When he stepped over the edge, miles of air under

his black slipper
out on the no-
cable joining the
scrapers—which
and flexing the
groaned so
it throw him
he swayed
how many mile-
were blowing off
than a hundred stories
Manhattan, passersby,
workers looking
could breathe? Seven
back: He knelt.
On his last
walked to the center
his back. The crowd
honked. After
to be one) he was—
"Take it easy," a cop said,
an artist."
behind, another
a stairway. The judge
to walk the high
for free, but over
Park, where he delighted
Philippe Petit, this
black, just before
sky, kneeling
one fist, the high

shoe, and walked
thicker-than-a-thumb
World Trade sky
moved, changing
wire, which itself
animal like (Would
off?)—surely
up there. I don't know
an-hour gusts
the Atlantic, more
above Lower
shoppers, office
up, staring. Who
times over and
He ran. He pranced.
crossing, Philippe
and lay down on
ooohed, taxis
(and there has
o yes, arrested.
"this man's
Cuffing his hands
pushed him down
sentenced him
wire, again
Lake Belvedere, in Central
thousands. Imagine,
little guy in
coming in out of the
on the cable and lifting
wire walker's salute.

Shhusssssssss

sssssss!s—steel
edge/to/ice/edge

d

o

w   up

n

over
the world
between outstretched arms

below
trees like dark fur
on a small
bear
so
still
closeby gray barkblur&Sun
-lightflash-
ing
the distance
still
and clear
clear as a
tink
of ice
across the blue
snow mountain

air

Caffe Solé

North Beach, San Francisco

Morning sun
  is shining.
    is shining.
          Maria,
at the Trieste, on upper Grant,
                    is serving cappaccino, caffe latte, espresso.
"La donna e mobile,"
          "Bella figlia dell amore," play on the jukebox.

                It is
Sunday, tabletops blaze with reflected light,
and air breathes through the walls.
People walk in and out through the open sun-filled doorway.
They sit at their ease and read newspapers,
some sit and talk,
others sit alone, sipping coffee.
Men in shirt sleeves,
              women with hair worn freely,
they enter
        and walk to the counter,
Gino presses levers on the chrome-and-red coffee machine,
and Maria serves caffe latte or cappuccino or espresso.
Someone is singing, *"La donna e mobile,"*
light fills the empty porcelain cups,
the sun is shining
             —it is Sunday
morning, and Caffe Trieste is like a canary cage
when the cover is lifted.

i to i

"(once like a spark)
if strangers meet
life begins . . ."
—*e.e. cummings*

always I was too shy
to ring his doorbell.
I feared admiration
would cling like honey, sealing
me dumb. I could not sing
"onetwothreefourfive pigeonsjustlikethat"
under his window
the way Vassar girls were said to do
every spring. Yet
we had one chance
meeting. He was walking
east on 8th, while I
was advancing west.
He looked enough unlike him
self to confuse, and I stared—
It was a spark he caught
and threw back, like a kid
playing with a mirror.
And we passed, each
turning as we walked
until both walking backward
were for a moment
eye to eye.

All the Way Clanging the Bell

Doc Eddie got out of medical school & up the next morning
  in the still dark his black leather doctor's bag flying
      dashed off & hollered down a trolley car between stations
Alone he & the conductor speeding the line from South Brooklyn to Flatbush
     him clanging the trolley bell loudly all the way
And without a stop got there
     in time to help deliver a new day

On his way again 8 a.m.
    Gravesend Mosholu Sunnyside Clasons Point Red Hook Rockaway Flushing
      two hours at the local clinic two hospital visits nine house calls
      then home to a waiting room full
       tending to three colds one fracture two diathermies & a blood test

In his hands held the hands of the lonely the troubled the dying
  ministering their toothaches headaches backaches heartaches
     his counsel steady unhurried true as the breathsound in a stethoscope

Annunziato Bartochowski Chen Calamaras Greenberg Kubota Zaryckj
  five boroughs of sixty flights of stairs every daynight
     for forty years he took care of them all
Going to the movies eating supper & to bed somewhere in time
  for several hours sleep when the telephone
     sounding scared & said he'd better come quick
Hurry he ran with his shirttails out
  flapping & flagged down the Avenue A Trolley

Rode all the way clanging the bell
  & never once got off till he reached the end of the line

Mom Gets In One of My Poems

"I thought I missed you, darling," she is saying on the phone.
"No, you woke me. It's 7:30."
"Oh—" she says, and then,
after a pause, "I didn't want to miss you."

How she won't be denied, how
I resist. Ninety-two, she's the kind
of goodness brings trouble, the powerful
voice calling me in

                evenings when I was a boy.
Maybe now it's her way
          to know she is okay.
Yesterday she called four times

for help with the date, days of the week
refusing to stay in their places.
"It's Saturday," she says, a questioning in her voice, adding,
"I'm so confused, it's embarrassing."

I can see her calendar: she's crossed off Friday
and forgotten, now maybe Saturday, too.
"I'm sorry, I cause you so much trouble," she says, starting to cry.
"It's okay, Ma, I mix up days, too.

              Last week," I tell her,
"I drove to the wrong job."
              Suddenly she laughs,
and I know it's okay, for the moment
neither hearing the powerful voice.

Spring Forward

Open the windows.
Everyone in the house is happier. The house
is happier, fresh air
in our mouths—finally. Purple finches
sing on the telephone wire, one finch singing
out his scarlet brains. Everyone
is happier, even the chair
beside the window, the cat
in the chair more possessed of the moment
than Buddha. All the windows are open,
coffee is up, and you laugh, pointing—
"The groundhog's out!"

Call Into Evening

> "We live in an old chaos of the sun,
> unsponsored, free."
> —*Wallace Stevens*

Tall pine trees all the way
    down to the stone shoreline. There's
        a cedar dock, its boards warped
           and silver in sunlight.

A foghorn, who knows why,
    because white paint is so clear on some lobster buoys
        in this early spring, lowering sun,
           already behind a stand of pines, darkness

gathering below, the shadows
    lengthening toward me.
        Everything else is lighting up,
           especially young leaves, light shining green

through them; and dandelions, the sun
    igniting their golden tops;
        the sides of a few white birches
           lighting up, and a ladder

near the dock, sun hitting
    at such an angle
        rungs are ingots of light.
           And something about the foghorn

sings—What? wildness, stones
      and blue water, the endless march of pines, dark green
            hackles of them against the sky,
                  inexplicably all so moving.

You know, I've already lived a life—done this
      I don't know how many times—and am amazed
            everything is so young, the moment undeniably
                  redolent in this green needle sun, even as it lowers

like—Oh, everything gone, gone like smoke, god knows where.
      And I remember once hearing some physicist
            say life must be universal
                through our whole astronomical system, something

I've known always anyway, and then
      something else about how
            someday we arrive where we started and know the place
            for the first time.

And I am amazed how neatly
      sewn together we are, the way
            everything fits through my eye, moving through
            all the senses—it all in me,

me in it—all of us
      this breathing, cosmic blossom, opening,
            closing in the vast sea of lightyears.
            A breeze, and I feel the chill.

Fence shadows lean out across the road, light reddening
    like the rust on two abandoned cars. The foghorn
        again. Some ducks start up, slapping water, lift
            and call into evening.

Improvisation

Haystack Mountain School of Crafts, 30 September 2000

I'm not going to talk anymore, I'm going to sit here in the September
Haystack sun and play my flute and not speak, not a word.
I'll be a sunshine man in this all blue September day, the sky
blue, the sea blue, all around blue except of course evergreens
and avocado-rind green blue spruce, saw-edged against sky blue
sea and sea blue sky. "Sweet Jesuz," a friend says over my shoulder,
"I am old," crooning it a way that doesn't sound like dying but shines
just like the steptop sun silver Haystack deck, only not a word—
I'm not saying a one. I sit atop the stackhay decklong flights of stairs
above the sea, high as osprey circling this topstep Sun, improvising
my blue Indian flutesong, two flags snap-snapping in seachop wind like
the shoe rag in a black man's hands I was jealous how he made
sing, just the way my friend who said "Sweet Jesuz" made the word old
sing like silver deckboards here in the Deer Isle morning. No, I'm not
talking anymore, I'll be the shine man, snapping his September rag on
my yellow birch flute, Sun so bright day goes white down the long and
open, silver Haystack stairs, improvising Sweet Jesuz, sing! who be old.

Acknowledgements & Notes

Acknowledgements are due to the editors of the following publications, in whose pages some of the poems in this book first appeared.

"A Bell"—The American Voice
"All the Way Clanging the Bell"—The Ohio Review
"Anonymous"—The New York Times
"Awake"—Berkeley Poets Cooperative Magazine
"Brother"—Maine in Print
"Brothers of Morning Brush My Eyes"—Potato Eyes
"*Caffe Solé*"—The Humanist, under the title "North Beach, San Francisco"
"Call Into Evening"—Borderlands: Texas Poetry Review
"China, Maine"—Best Poems 1986 North Eastern States Poetry Contest
"Fishing"—The American Poetry Review
"For the Moment"—Maine Times
"I Keep Thinking of You, Victor Jara"—The American Poetry Review
"i To i "—Berkeley Poets Cooperative 24
"Improvisation"—Rattle
"In Response"—Puckerbrush Review
"Love Canal"—Berkeley Poets Cooperative 21
"Money Medicine Poem"—Amelia #2
                    (Winner of The Margurette Cummins Quarterly Broadside Award)
"Night Letters"—Red Brick Review
"Out of the Blue"—Maine Times &The Comstock Review
"Painting 101"—The Beloit Poetry Journal
"Red Dust"—Hubbub
"Shofar"—Puerto del Sol
"Skydreaming a Sunny Afternoon in Portland, a Small City"—Maine Times
"Shhsssssssss"—Milkweed Editions & University of Iowa Press
"Spring Forward"—The Amicus Journal
"Stilt Dancing the Penacook Valley Parade in What Must Be Heaven"—The Progressive
"The Disappeared"—Best Poems 1985 Northeastern States Poetry Contest
"The Three"—The American Poetry Review
"This is a Safe House"—Witness
"Those Pelicans"—Borderlands: Texas Poetry Review
"Whatever You Want"—Maine Times
"Wild Geese"—Blueline
"Woman Behind the Wheel, in Sunlight" —Borderlands: Texas Poetry Review

Unbounded Thanks to Harriet Barlow and Blue Mountain Center
for the Arts for their gift of friendship, encouragement, support
and the time to work on many of the poems in this book.
&
Thanks to the Maine Arts Commission and the community of
writers, artists and other friends here, like Wesley McNair, Baron
Wormser, Betsy Sholl, Carl Dimow, Candice Stover, Chris Queally,
Vivian Walter, Richard Willing, Sarah Cecil, Samuel Cordeiro, Lisa
Hicks, Lisa Newcomb, Eleni Koenka, Jeffrey Haste, and Gary Bennett,
whose caring, interest and support sustains and continues to nourish me.
—*Martin Steingesser*

AUTHOR'S NOTES

page 34 * Koleba, a blend word of the children's three names and of the
Czechoslovakian words *koleda*, a children's fairytale, and *chleba*, bread.

page 35 * Love Canal was a half-mile trench in Niagara Falls, where Hooker Chemical
Company buried tons of chemical waste throughout the 1960's and 70's, causing one of
the first pollution disasters to break into national consciousness.

"So many cancers are still happening on the street,"a former resident of the community
near Love Canal said in a radio interview 20 years after the area was declared a disaster.

"They landscape, but it's always brown there," she said. "You can smell it from my
parents' house, so metallic whenever wind blows in the right direction."

Hooker Chemical Company, owned by Occidental Chemical, was renamed Secos.

Martin Steingesser grew up and lived on New York City's Lower East Side, moving to
Maine in 1981. Also a performance poet, he works actively both presenting and teaching
in the Maine Arts Commission's Touring Artist and Artist-in-Residence programs. His
poems have garnered national recognition, and he has been a Fellow of Blue Mountain
Center for the Arts and recipient of the University of Southern Maine's Stonecoast
Writers' Conference Pierre Menard Poetry Scholarship.

He says writing is a way he touches and makes present a sense of grace he wants in his
life: "There are moments in poems I have made—when they are given, when windows,
doors, walls are blown off, and I am in a warm, boundless space with whoever is
listening."

Cover photograph by Roger Haile.

This photo was taken by Roger in 1985 at Matagalpa, Nicaragua, while engaged in a
project with several other photographers teaching black and white photography skills.